Table of Contents

Chapter 1: Introduction to AI Applications in Agriculture 3
    What is Artificial Intelligence? 3
    The Role of AI in Agriculture 4
    Benefits of AI in Farming 4
Chapter 2: Crop Monitoring and Management 5
    Remote Sensing Technologies 5
    Satellite Imagery Analysis 6
    Drones in Crop Monitoring 6
Chapter 3: Precision Agriculture 7
    Precision Planting 7
    Variable Rate Technology 8
    Precision Fertilization 9
Chapter 4: Pest and Disease Detection 10
    Early Pest Detection 10
    Disease Identification Algorithms 10
    Integrated Pest Management 11
Chapter 5: Livestock Monitoring and Management 12
    Health Monitoring Systems 12
    Automated Feeding Solutions 13
    Livestock Tracking Technologies 13
Chapter 6: Soil Health Analysis 14
    Soil Sensors 14
    Soil Sampling Techniques 15
    Nutrient Management Systems 16
Chapter 7: Automated Harvesting and Sorting 16
    Robotic Harvesters 16
    Automated Sorting Machines 17
    Post-Harvest Quality Control 18
Chapter 8: Irrigation Management 19
    Smart Irrigation Systems 19
    Soil Moisture Sensors 19
    Drip Irrigation Technology 20
Chapter 9: Weather Forecasting and Crop Prediction 21

- **Weather Data Analytics** 21
- **Climate Prediction Models** 22
- **Crop Yield Forecasting** 23

Chapter 10: Crop Yield Optimization 23
- **Yield Prediction Models** 23
- **Crop Growth Simulations** 24
- **Crop Rotation Strategies** 25

Chapter 11: Supply Chain Management and Logistics in Agriculture 26
- **Traceability Systems** 26
- **Real-Time Inventory Management** 26
- **Transportation Optimization** 27

Chapter 12: Conclusion 28
- **Future Trends in AI Applications in Agriculture** 28
- **Challenges and Opportunities in AgTech** 29
- **The Impact of AI on the Future of Farming** 30

Chapter 1: Introduction to AI Applications in Agriculture

What is Artificial Intelligence?

Artificial Intelligence, or AI, is a rapidly advancing technology that is revolutionizing various industries, including agriculture. In the context of farming, AI refers to the use of advanced algorithms and machine learning techniques to analyze data and make informed decisions. By harnessing the power of AI, farmers can improve crop monitoring and management, enhance precision agriculture practices, detect pests and diseases early, monitor and manage livestock more effectively, analyze soil health, automate harvesting and sorting processes, optimize irrigation management, predict weather patterns and crop yields, and streamline supply chain management and logistics in agriculture.

One of the key applications of AI in agriculture is crop monitoring and management. Through the use of AI-powered drones and sensors, farmers can collect real-time data on crop health, growth rates, and environmental conditions. This information allows farmers to make data-driven decisions on when to plant, fertilize, and harvest crops, leading to increased yields and improved sustainability. Additionally, AI can help farmers identify and address issues such as nutrient deficiencies, pest infestations, and water stress before they become major problems.

Precision agriculture is another area where AI is making a significant impact. By using AI algorithms to analyze data from satellites, drones, and sensors, farmers can create highly detailed maps of their fields, enabling them to apply fertilizers, pesticides, and water only where and when they are needed. This not only reduces waste and environmental impact but also improves crop yields and profitability. AI can also be used to optimize planting patterns, monitor crop growth, and predict harvest times with greater accuracy.

Pest and disease detection is another critical application of AI in agriculture. By analyzing images of crops taken by drones or cameras, AI algorithms can identify early signs of pest infestations or diseases, allowing farmers to take proactive measures to prevent crop losses. Additionally, AI can help farmers monitor livestock health and behavior, detect signs of illness or distress, and optimize feeding schedules and breeding practices.

Soil health analysis is another area where AI is proving to be invaluable. By analyzing soil samples and environmental data, AI algorithms can provide farmers with insights into soil nutrient levels, pH levels, moisture content, and other factors that affect crop growth. This information can help farmers make informed decisions on soil management practices, such as fertilization, irrigation, and crop rotation, leading to improved soil health and higher crop yields.

In conclusion, AI has the potential to revolutionize the agriculture industry by enabling farmers to make smarter, more data-driven decisions. From crop monitoring and management to precision agriculture, pest and disease detection, livestock monitoring, soil health analysis, automated harvesting, and sorting, irrigation management, weather forecasting, crop prediction, yield optimization, and supply chain management, AI is transforming every aspect of farming.

By embracing this technology, farmers can increase productivity, reduce costs, minimize environmental impact, and ensure a sustainable future for agriculture.

The Role of AI in Agriculture

In recent years, the role of artificial intelligence (AI) in agriculture has become increasingly prominent. AI applications in agriculture have revolutionized the way farmers monitor and manage their crops, leading to increased efficiency and productivity. From crop monitoring and management to pest and disease detection, AI technology is helping farmers make more informed decisions to optimize their yield and reduce waste.

Precision agriculture is one area where AI is making a significant impact. By using drones, sensors, and other advanced technologies, farmers can now gather precise data about their fields, such as soil moisture levels and nutrient content. This information allows farmers to tailor their farming practices to the specific needs of each crop, leading to higher yields and reduced environmental impact.

Another key area where AI is transforming agriculture is in pest and disease detection. By using machine learning algorithms, farmers can quickly identify and treat potential threats to their crops, minimizing the need for harmful pesticides and saving valuable resources. AI technology can also help farmers monitor and manage their livestock more effectively, ensuring the health and well-being of their animals.

Soil health analysis is another important application of AI in agriculture. By analyzing soil samples and other data, farmers can better understand the nutrient levels and overall health of their soil. This information can help farmers make informed decisions about fertilization and irrigation, leading to healthier crops and improved yield.

Overall, the role of AI in agriculture is rapidly expanding, with applications ranging from automated harvesting and sorting to irrigation management and weather forecasting. By harnessing the power of AI technology, farmers can optimize their crop yield, improve supply chain management, and enhance the overall efficiency and sustainability of their operations. As the future of farming continues to evolve, AI applications in agriculture will play an increasingly vital role in ensuring food security and environmental sustainability.

Benefits of AI in Farming

AI applications in agriculture have revolutionized the way farmers approach crop monitoring and management. With the help of AI technology, farmers can now track the growth and health of their crops in real-time, allowing them to make informed decisions about irrigation, fertilization, and pest control. This has resulted in higher crop yields and reduced waste, ultimately leading to increased profits for farmers.

Precision agriculture is another area where AI has made a significant impact. By using drones and sensors equipped with AI algorithms, farmers can now create detailed maps of their fields and identify areas that require special attention. This targeted approach to farming has led to more efficient use of resources such as water and fertilizers, as well as improved crop quality.

Pest and disease detection is a crucial aspect of farming that can be time-consuming and challenging for farmers to manage. AI technology has made this process much easier by enabling the use of image recognition software to identify pests and diseases in crops. By detecting these issues early on, farmers can take quick action to prevent further damage and ensure the health of their crops.

Livestock monitoring and management have also benefited from AI applications in agriculture. By using wearable sensors and AI algorithms, farmers can now track the health and behavior of their animals more effectively. This data allows for early detection of any health issues and helps farmers optimize their livestock management practices for better overall productivity.

In conclusion, the benefits of AI in farming are vast and continue to grow as technology advances. From soil health analysis to automated harvesting and sorting, AI is transforming the way farmers operate and improving the efficiency and sustainability of agriculture. By embracing AI applications in agriculture, farmers can optimize their crop yields, reduce waste, and ensure the health and well-being of their livestock, ultimately leading to a more profitable and sustainable future for the agricultural industry.

Chapter 2: Crop Monitoring and Management

Remote Sensing Technologies

Remote sensing technologies play a crucial role in the advancement of AI applications in agriculture. These technologies involve collecting data from a distance, using satellites, drones, and other devices to monitor and manage crops more efficiently. By utilizing remote sensing technologies, farmers can gather valuable information about their fields, such as crop health, soil moisture levels, and pest infestations, without having to physically inspect every inch of their land.

One of the main benefits of remote sensing technologies is the ability to conduct crop monitoring and management on a large scale. With the use of drones equipped with sensors, farmers can quickly identify areas of their fields that require attention, such as areas experiencing drought stress or pest damage. This real-time data allows farmers to make informed decisions about irrigation, fertilization, and pest control, ultimately improving crop yields and reducing waste.

Precision agriculture is another area where remote sensing technologies shine. By collecting detailed data on soil health, moisture levels, and crop growth, farmers can create customized treatment plans for each section of their fields. This targeted approach not only improves efficiency but also reduces the environmental impact of farming practices by minimizing the use of chemicals and water.

In addition to crop monitoring and management, remote sensing technologies are also used for pest and disease detection. By analyzing images captured by drones or satellites, farmers can identify early signs of infestations or diseases, allowing them to take swift action to prevent widespread damage. This proactive approach can save farmers time and money, as well as protect their crops from devastation.

Overall, remote sensing technologies are revolutionizing the way farmers approach agriculture. By harnessing the power of AI and data analytics, farmers can make more informed decisions about their crops, leading to increased productivity and sustainability. As technology continues to advance, the possibilities for remote sensing in agriculture are endless, paving the way for a more efficient and environmentally-friendly future in farming.

Satellite Imagery Analysis

Satellite Imagery Analysis is a crucial component of AI applications in agriculture, as it allows farmers to monitor their crops from a bird's eye view. By analyzing images captured by satellites, farmers can gain valuable insights into the health and growth of their crops, helping them make informed decisions about when to water, fertilize, or harvest. This technology has revolutionized crop monitoring and management, allowing farmers to optimize their yields and reduce waste.

Precision agriculture relies heavily on satellite imagery analysis to create detailed maps of fields and monitor crop health on a large scale. By using AI algorithms to analyze satellite images, farmers can pinpoint areas of fields that need attention, such as where pests or diseases are present, or where irrigation is needed. This targeted approach not only saves time and resources but also minimizes environmental impact by reducing the need for excess fertilizers or pesticides.

Pest and disease detection have also been greatly enhanced by satellite imagery analysis. By monitoring changes in vegetation patterns over time, AI algorithms can detect early signs of pest infestations or disease outbreaks, allowing farmers to take swift action to protect their crops. This technology has the potential to save farmers millions of dollars in lost yields and prevent the spread of harmful pathogens.

Livestock monitoring and management have also benefited from satellite imagery analysis. By tracking the movement and behavior of animals from above, farmers can ensure the health and well-being of their livestock, as well as optimize grazing patterns and feeding schedules. This technology has the potential to improve animal welfare standards and increase overall productivity in the livestock industry.

In conclusion, satellite imagery analysis is a powerful tool in the arsenal of AI applications in agriculture. By harnessing the data captured by satellites, farmers can make more informed decisions about crop management, pest control, livestock monitoring, and more. This technology has the potential to revolutionize the way we approach farming, leading to higher yields, reduced waste, and a more sustainable agricultural industry.

Drones in Crop Monitoring

Drones have revolutionized the way farmers monitor their crops, providing valuable insights into crop health and overall field conditions. These unmanned aerial vehicles equipped with high-resolution cameras and sensors can capture detailed images of crops, allowing farmers to identify areas of concern such as pest infestations, nutrient deficiencies, or water stress. By using drones in crop monitoring, farmers can make informed decisions about when and where to apply pesticides, fertilizers, or irrigation, ultimately increasing crop yield and reducing input costs.

Precision agriculture is a key aspect of using drones in crop monitoring, as it allows farmers to target specific areas of their fields that require attention. By analyzing the data collected by drones, farmers can create prescription maps that guide them in applying inputs precisely where they are needed, reducing waste and environmental impact. This targeted approach to crop management not only improves crop health but also maximizes resource efficiency, making farming operations more sustainable in the long run.

In addition to monitoring crop health, drones can also be used to detect pests and diseases early on, before they cause significant damage to crops. By flying drones over fields on a regular basis, farmers can quickly identify any signs of pest infestations or disease outbreaks and take immediate action to mitigate the problem. This proactive approach to pest and disease management can prevent widespread crop losses and ensure a healthy harvest at the end of the season.

Livestock monitoring and management is another area where drones are being increasingly used in agriculture. Drones equipped with thermal imaging cameras can help farmers track the movement and health of their livestock, ensuring that animals are well cared for and identifying any potential issues before they escalate. By using drones for livestock management, farmers can improve animal welfare, increase productivity, and ultimately enhance their overall farm operations.

Overall, drones play a crucial role in modern agriculture, offering farmers valuable insights into their crops, livestock, and overall field conditions. By incorporating drones into their crop monitoring and management practices, farmers can make more informed decisions, optimize resource use, and ultimately increase their profitability. As technology continues to advance, the potential applications of drones in agriculture are limitless, offering exciting opportunities for farmers to improve their operations and embrace the future of farming.

Chapter 3: Precision Agriculture

Precision Planting

Precision planting is a crucial aspect of modern agriculture that utilizes AI applications to enhance crop production and efficiency. By employing advanced technologies such as GPS, sensors, and machine learning algorithms, farmers can precisely plant seeds at optimal depths and spacing to ensure maximum yield. This precision planting technique not only improves crop quality but also reduces input costs and minimizes environmental impact.

One of the key benefits of precision planting is the ability to customize seed placement based on soil conditions, moisture levels, and other environmental factors. By analyzing data collected from sensors and satellites, farmers can make informed decisions about where and when to plant each seed, resulting in uniform growth and better overall crop health. This level of precision allows for efficient use of resources and ultimately leads to higher yields and profitability for farmers.

In addition to improving crop production, precision planting also plays a significant role in sustainable agriculture practices. By optimizing seed placement and reducing waste, farmers can minimize the use of pesticides, fertilizers, and water, leading to a more environmentally friendly farming operation. This approach not only benefits the environment but also helps farmers meet the growing demand for sustainable and ethically produced food.

Furthermore, AI applications in precision planting can help farmers monitor and manage their crops more effectively. By continuously collecting data on plant growth, soil health, and weather conditions, farmers can make timely adjustments to their planting strategies to optimize crop performance. This real-time monitoring and analysis enable farmers to identify issues such as pest infestations or nutrient deficiencies early on and take corrective action before significant damage occurs.

Overall, precision planting is a vital component of modern agriculture that leverages AI technologies to improve crop production, reduce environmental impact, and enhance sustainability. By adopting precision planting techniques, farmers can achieve higher yields, lower costs, and greater efficiency in their operations. As the agriculture industry continues to evolve, precision planting will play an increasingly important role in meeting the global demand for food while ensuring the long-term viability of our planet.

Variable Rate Technology

Variable Rate Technology (VRT) is a key component of precision agriculture that utilizes AI applications to optimize crop production. By analyzing data collected from various sources such as satellite imagery, soil sensors, and weather forecasts, VRT allows farmers to tailor their inputs such as fertilizers, pesticides, and water according to the specific needs of different areas within a field. This targeted approach not only improves crop yields but also minimizes input wastage and environmental impact.

One of the main advantages of VRT is its ability to monitor and manage crops in real-time. Through the use of AI algorithms, farmers can receive alerts and recommendations on when and where to apply inputs based on factors like soil moisture levels, nutrient content, and pest infestations. This proactive approach helps farmers to address issues before they become significant problems, leading to healthier and more productive crops.

In addition to crop monitoring and management, VRT also plays a crucial role in pest and disease detection. By analyzing data from sensors and drones, AI algorithms can identify early signs of pests or diseases in crops, allowing farmers to take immediate action to prevent further damage. This early detection not only saves crops but also reduces the need for chemical treatments, resulting in cost savings and environmental benefits.

Livestock monitoring and management is another area where VRT can make a significant impact. By using AI-powered sensors and tracking devices, farmers can monitor the health and behavior of individual animals in real-time. This data can help farmers identify signs of illness or distress early on, enabling them to provide timely treatment and improve overall animal welfare.

Overall, VRT is revolutionizing agriculture by enabling farmers to make data-driven decisions that optimize crop production, minimize environmental impact, and improve overall efficiency. As AI technology continues to advance, the potential for VRT to further enhance crop yield optimization, supply chain management, and logistics in agriculture is vast. By embracing these innovations, farmers can not only increase their profitability but also contribute to a more sustainable and resilient food system for the future.

Precision Fertilization

Precision fertilization is a key component of precision agriculture, which utilizes advanced technologies like artificial intelligence to optimize crop production. By using AI applications in agriculture, farmers can now analyze soil composition, crop requirements, and environmental factors to determine the exact amount of nutrients needed for each individual crop. This targeted approach minimizes waste and ensures that crops receive the necessary nutrients for optimal growth and yield.

Crop monitoring and management play a crucial role in precision fertilization. AI-powered sensors and drones can collect real-time data on crop health, growth stages, and nutrient levels, allowing farmers to make informed decisions about fertilization schedules. By integrating this data with AI algorithms, farmers can create customized fertilization plans that address the specific needs of each crop, leading to increased efficiency and productivity.

Pest and disease detection is another important aspect of precision fertilization. By using AI applications in agriculture, farmers can identify potential pest and disease threats early on, allowing for timely intervention and prevention. This proactive approach not only protects crops from damage but also ensures that fertilization efforts are not wasted on plants that may not survive due to pest infestations.

Livestock monitoring and management also benefit from precision fertilization practices. By using AI technologies to track animal health, feed intake, and nutrient requirements, farmers can optimize their livestock feeding programs to ensure optimal growth and health. This results in higher-quality meat and dairy products while minimizing the environmental impact of livestock farming.

Overall, precision fertilization is a game-changer in modern agriculture, thanks to the advancements in AI applications. By leveraging technology to analyze data, monitor crops and livestock, and make informed decisions, farmers can maximize their yields, minimize waste, and contribute to sustainable agriculture practices. As the future of farming continues to evolve, precision fertilization will undoubtedly play a crucial role in feeding a growing population while preserving our natural resources.

Chapter 4: Pest and Disease Detection

Early Pest Detection

Early pest detection is a crucial aspect of modern agriculture, as it allows farmers to identify and address potential issues before they have a chance to spread and cause significant damage to crops. With the help of AI applications, farmers can now monitor their fields in real-time and receive alerts when pests are detected, enabling them to take swift action to protect their crops.

One of the key benefits of using AI for pest detection is its ability to identify pests at an early stage, often before they are visible to the naked eye. By analyzing data collected from sensors and drones, AI algorithms can detect subtle changes in plant health that may indicate the presence of pests. This early detection allows farmers to implement targeted pest control measures, minimizing the need for chemical pesticides and reducing the overall environmental impact of farming practices.

In addition to early detection, AI applications in agriculture can also help farmers to monitor pest populations over time and track their movements across fields. By analyzing data on pest behavior and population dynamics, farmers can gain valuable insights into the most effective strategies for pest control and management. This data-driven approach can help farmers to optimize their pest control efforts and reduce the risk of crop damage.

Furthermore, AI applications can be used to predict and prevent pest outbreaks before they occur. By analyzing historical data on pest populations, weather patterns, and crop health, AI algorithms can identify potential risk factors for pest infestations and provide early warnings to farmers. This proactive approach to pest management can help farmers to avoid costly crop losses and maintain healthy yields throughout the growing season.

Overall, early pest detection is a critical component of precision agriculture, allowing farmers to protect their crops more effectively and sustainably. By harnessing the power of AI applications, farmers can leverage real-time data and advanced analytics to detect, monitor, and control pests with greater precision and efficiency. As the agriculture industry continues to embrace AI technologies, early pest detection will play an increasingly important role in optimizing crop yields and ensuring food security for future generations.

Disease Identification Algorithms

Disease Identification Algorithms play a crucial role in modern agriculture by utilizing artificial intelligence to detect and diagnose diseases in crops and livestock. These algorithms use advanced technology to analyze data collected from sensors and cameras to identify signs of diseases early on, allowing farmers to take prompt action to prevent the spread of diseases and minimize crop or livestock loss.

One of the key benefits of Disease Identification Algorithms is their ability to accurately and quickly detect diseases in crops and livestock. By analyzing various data points such as temperature, humidity, and images of plants or animals, these algorithms can identify patterns and indicators of diseases that may not be visible to the naked eye. This early detection is essential for farmers to implement targeted treatments and prevent the spread of diseases to other crops or animals.

Precision agriculture is one of the niches within AI applications in agriculture that heavily relies on Disease Identification Algorithms. By integrating these algorithms into precision agriculture systems, farmers can monitor their crops and livestock in real-time and receive alerts when diseases are detected. This proactive approach allows farmers to take immediate action, such as adjusting irrigation or applying pesticides, to prevent the spread of diseases and ensure the health and productivity of their crops and livestock.

In addition to crop monitoring and management, Disease Identification Algorithms are also used in livestock monitoring and management. By analyzing data from sensors attached to animals, these algorithms can detect signs of diseases such as fever or abnormal behavior, enabling farmers to provide timely treatment and prevent the spread of diseases within their livestock. This proactive approach not only ensures the health and well-being of the animals but also helps farmers maintain productivity and profitability in their operations.

Overall, Disease Identification Algorithms are a powerful tool in modern agriculture that helps farmers improve disease management, reduce crop and livestock losses, and increase overall productivity. By leveraging advanced technology and artificial intelligence, farmers can detect diseases early, implement targeted treatments, and prevent the spread of diseases to ensure the health and success of their crops and livestock. As technology continues to advance, Disease Identification Algorithms will play an increasingly important role in shaping the future of farming and agriculture.

Integrated Pest Management

Integrated Pest Management (IPM) is a crucial aspect of modern agriculture, especially in the age of AI applications. IPM involves the use of various techniques to manage pests in a way that minimizes risks to human health, the environment, and the economy. AI applications have revolutionized IPM by providing farmers with advanced tools and technologies to monitor, detect, and combat pests effectively.

One of the key benefits of AI applications in IPM is crop monitoring and management. Through the use of drones, satellites, and sensors, farmers can collect real-time data on crop health and pest infestations. This data allows farmers to make informed decisions about pest control strategies, such as the use of biological controls or targeted pesticide applications.

Precision agriculture, another niche of AI applications in agriculture, plays a vital role in IPM. By using AI algorithms and machine learning, farmers can identify pest hotspots and target interventions more effectively. This targeted approach not only reduces the use of harmful chemicals but also increases the overall effectiveness of pest management strategies.

Pest and disease detection is another area where AI applications shine in IPM. By analyzing images and data collected from sensors, AI algorithms can quickly identify signs of pest infestations or diseases in crops. This early detection allows farmers to take immediate action to prevent the spread of pests and diseases, ultimately reducing crop losses and increasing yields.

Overall, the integration of AI applications in IPM has revolutionized the way farmers manage pests and diseases in their crops. By leveraging advanced technologies such as drones, sensors, and machine learning algorithms, farmers can implement more sustainable and effective pest management strategies. As the agriculture industry continues to evolve, the role of AI in IPM will only become more critical in ensuring the future of farming is sustainable and productive.

Chapter 5: Livestock Monitoring and Management

Health Monitoring Systems

Health monitoring systems are a crucial component of modern agriculture, allowing farmers to track the well-being of their crops and livestock in real-time. These systems utilize advanced technologies such as AI and IoT sensors to collect data on various health indicators, including plant growth, nutrient levels, disease presence, and animal behavior. By providing farmers with detailed insights into the health of their agricultural assets, these monitoring systems enable more proactive and targeted management practices.

Crop monitoring and management is one of the key applications of health monitoring systems in agriculture. By continuously monitoring factors such as soil moisture, temperature, and nutrient levels, farmers can optimize their crop management practices to ensure maximum yield and quality. AI-powered algorithms analyze the data collected by these monitoring systems to provide recommendations for irrigation, fertilization, and pest control, helping farmers make informed decisions to protect and enhance their crops.

Precision agriculture is another area where health monitoring systems play a vital role. By combining data from multiple sources, including satellite imagery, weather forecasts, and soil sensors, these systems enable farmers to create highly detailed maps of their fields and tailor their management practices to specific areas. This precision approach allows for more efficient resource use, reduced environmental impact, and increased crop yields.

Pest and disease detection is a critical aspect of health monitoring systems in agriculture, helping farmers identify and address potential threats before they cause significant damage. By monitoring factors such as plant health, pest populations, and weather conditions, these systems can detect early signs of infestations or infections and alert farmers to take appropriate action. AI algorithms can analyze this data to identify patterns and predict future outbreaks, enabling proactive pest and disease management strategies.

Livestock monitoring and management is an essential application of health monitoring systems for animal agriculture. By tracking parameters such as animal behavior, feed intake, and health indicators, farmers can ensure the well-being of their livestock and optimize production efficiency. These systems can also provide early warning signs of disease outbreaks or welfare issues, allowing farmers to take prompt action to prevent losses and maintain the health of their animals.

Automated Feeding Solutions

Automated Feeding Solutions play a crucial role in modern agriculture, especially in livestock monitoring and management. With the advancement of AI applications in agriculture, farmers can now benefit from automated feeding systems that ensure their livestock is fed efficiently and accurately. These systems use sensors to monitor the animals' feeding patterns and adjust the feed accordingly, leading to improved animal health and increased productivity.

One of the key advantages of Automated Feeding Solutions is the ability to provide individualized feeding plans for each animal based on their specific nutritional needs. By using AI algorithms to analyze data collected from sensors, farmers can create custom feeding schedules that optimize the animals' growth and health. This not only improves the overall well-being of the livestock but also reduces feed wastage and costs for the farmer.

Furthermore, Automated Feeding Solutions help farmers save time and labor by automating the feeding process. Instead of manually feeding each animal, farmers can rely on automated systems to dispense the right amount of feed at the right time. This not only increases efficiency but also allows farmers to focus on other important tasks on the farm.

In addition to individualized feeding plans and labor savings, Automated Feeding Solutions also contribute to environmental sustainability in agriculture. By accurately measuring and dispensing feed, these systems help reduce waste and minimize the environmental impact of livestock farming. This is essential for meeting the growing demand for sustainable and ethical farming practices.

Overall, Automated Feeding Solutions are a valuable tool for farmers looking to optimize their livestock management practices. With the help of AI applications in agriculture, farmers can improve animal health, increase productivity, save time and labor, and contribute to environmental sustainability. By embracing these innovative technologies, farmers can stay ahead in the ever-evolving agricultural industry and ensure the future of farming is efficient, sustainable, and profitable.

Livestock Tracking Technologies

Livestock tracking technologies have revolutionized the way farmers manage their herds, providing valuable insights and data to improve overall efficiency and productivity. With the help of AI applications in agriculture, farmers can now monitor the health and well-being of their livestock in real-time, ensuring optimal conditions for growth and development.

One of the key benefits of livestock tracking technologies is the ability to monitor the location and movement of animals within a designated area. By using GPS technology and sensors attached to the animals, farmers can track their livestock's movements and behavior, allowing them to identify any potential issues or anomalies that may require attention. This level of monitoring is crucial for ensuring the safety and security of the animals, as well as optimizing feeding and grazing practices.

In addition to location tracking, livestock monitoring technologies also provide valuable data on the health and performance of individual animals. By analyzing factors such as heart rate, temperature, and activity levels, farmers can quickly identify any signs of illness or distress, allowing for prompt intervention and treatment. This proactive approach to livestock management can significantly reduce the risk of disease outbreaks and improve overall animal welfare.

Furthermore, AI applications in agriculture have enabled farmers to integrate livestock tracking data with other sources of information, such as weather forecasts and crop predictions. By analyzing this data in real-time, farmers can make more informed decisions about herd management, grazing patterns, and feed supplementation, ultimately leading to higher yields and profitability.

Overall, livestock tracking technologies are a valuable tool for farmers looking to optimize their operations and maximize the productivity of their herds. By harnessing the power of AI applications in agriculture, farmers can gain valuable insights into the health and performance of their livestock, leading to improved efficiency, sustainability, and profitability in the long run.

Chapter 6: Soil Health Analysis

Soil Sensors

Soil sensors are a crucial component of precision agriculture, allowing farmers to monitor and manage the health of their soil with great accuracy. These sensors are equipped with advanced technology that can measure key soil properties such as moisture levels, temperature, pH, and nutrient levels. By collecting this data in real-time, farmers can make informed decisions about irrigation, fertilization, and other soil management practices to optimize crop growth and yield.

One of the main benefits of soil sensors is their ability to provide farmers with detailed insights into the health of their soil. By continuously monitoring soil conditions, farmers can identify issues such as nutrient deficiencies, water stress, or pH imbalances before they have a negative impact on crop health. This proactive approach allows farmers to take corrective action in a timely manner, ultimately leading to healthier crops and higher yields.

In addition to monitoring soil health, soil sensors can also play a key role in pest and disease detection. By analyzing changes in soil moisture, temperature, and other key parameters, farmers can identify patterns that may indicate the presence of pests or diseases in their crops. This early detection can help farmers implement targeted interventions to prevent the spread of pests and diseases, saving both time and money in the long run.

Furthermore, soil sensors can be integrated with other technologies such as drones and AI algorithms to further enhance crop monitoring and management. By combining data from soil sensors with aerial imagery and machine learning algorithms, farmers can gain a more comprehensive understanding of their fields and make more informed decisions about crop management practices. This integrated approach to agriculture can help farmers optimize their crop yields while minimizing input costs and environmental impact.

Overall, soil sensors are a powerful tool for farmers who are looking to improve their soil health analysis and optimize their crop yields. By leveraging the latest advancements in technology, farmers can make smarter decisions about soil management, leading to more sustainable and profitable farming practices. As AI applications continue to advance in agriculture, soil sensors will play an increasingly important role in helping farmers meet the challenges of modern agriculture and ensure food security for future generations.

Soil Sampling Techniques

Soil sampling techniques play a crucial role in modern agriculture, especially when it comes to implementing AI applications in farming practices. By understanding the composition and health of the soil, farmers can make informed decisions about crop management, irrigation, and fertilization. This subchapter will explore various soil sampling techniques that are used in precision agriculture to optimize crop production and ensure sustainable farming practices.

One of the most common soil sampling techniques is grid sampling, where the field is divided into grids and soil samples are taken from each grid at regular intervals. This method allows farmers to identify variations in soil composition across the field and make targeted adjustments to improve crop yields. Another technique is zone sampling, where soil samples are taken from predetermined zones based on factors such as topography, soil type, and historical yield data. This approach helps farmers tailor their management practices to the specific needs of different areas within the field.

In addition to traditional soil sampling methods, AI applications are now being used to enhance soil health analysis. By analyzing data from sensors, drones, and satellite imagery, AI algorithms can provide real-time insights into soil moisture levels, nutrient levels, and compaction. This information allows farmers to make timely decisions about irrigation, fertilization, and tillage practices to optimize crop growth and minimize environmental impact.

Furthermore, AI applications in soil health analysis can help farmers detect nutrient deficiencies, pH imbalances, and other issues that may affect crop productivity. By monitoring soil health continuously, farmers can intervene early to prevent nutrient deficiencies and improve soil fertility over time. This proactive approach to soil management is essential for sustainable agriculture and long-term profitability.

Overall, soil sampling techniques are essential for implementing AI applications in agriculture and ensuring optimal crop production. By combining traditional sampling methods with cutting-edge technology, farmers can make data-driven decisions that lead to higher yields, healthier soils, and more sustainable farming practices. As the future of farming continues to evolve, soil health analysis will play a key role in maximizing crop productivity and preserving the environment for future generations.

Nutrient Management Systems

Nutrient management systems play a crucial role in modern agriculture, especially with the integration of AI applications. These systems are designed to optimize the use of nutrients such as nitrogen, phosphorus, and potassium in crop production, ensuring that plants receive the right amount of nutrients at the right time. AI technology has revolutionized nutrient management by providing farmers with real-time data on soil health, crop nutrient needs, and fertilizer application rates.

Crop monitoring and management are essential components of nutrient management systems. AI-powered sensors and drones are used to collect data on crop health, growth, and nutrient levels. This data is then analyzed by AI algorithms to provide farmers with insights into crop nutrient requirements and potential nutrient deficiencies. By using AI applications in crop monitoring and management, farmers can make informed decisions on fertilizer applications, leading to improved crop yields and reduced environmental impact.

Precision agriculture is another key aspect of nutrient management systems. This approach involves using AI technology to customize farming practices based on specific field conditions and crop requirements. By utilizing precision agriculture techniques, farmers can optimize the use of nutrients, reduce waste, and increase productivity. AI applications in precision agriculture enable farmers to monitor soil health, crop growth, and nutrient levels with precision, leading to more efficient nutrient management practices.

Pest and disease detection are also critical components of nutrient management systems. AI-powered sensors and imaging technology can detect early signs of pest infestations and diseases, allowing farmers to take proactive measures to protect their crops. By integrating pest and disease detection with nutrient management systems, farmers can address potential threats to crop health while optimizing nutrient applications to ensure optimal crop growth.

In conclusion, nutrient management systems are essential for sustainable agriculture, and AI applications have transformed the way farmers manage nutrients in their fields. By incorporating AI technology into crop monitoring and management, precision agriculture, pest and disease detection, and other aspects of nutrient management, farmers can optimize nutrient use, improve crop yields, and reduce environmental impact. The future of farming lies in the integration of AI applications in agriculture, and nutrient management systems are at the forefront of this technological revolution.

Chapter 7: Automated Harvesting and Sorting

Robotic Harvesters

Robotic harvesters are revolutionizing the way crops are collected in the agricultural industry. These advanced machines are equipped with artificial intelligence technology that allows them to efficiently and effectively harvest crops with precision and accuracy. By utilizing AI applications in agriculture, robotic harvesters can significantly increase productivity and reduce labor costs for farmers.

One of the key benefits of robotic harvesters is their ability to monitor and manage crops in real-time. These machines are equipped with sensors and cameras that can detect ripeness levels, diseases, and pests in crops. By continuously monitoring the health of crops, robotic harvesters can ensure that only the highest quality produce is harvested, leading to increased crop yields and profitability for farmers.

Precision agriculture is another area where robotic harvesters excel. These machines can navigate fields with precision and accuracy, ensuring that each crop is harvested at the optimal time and in the most efficient manner. By using AI algorithms, robotic harvesters can adjust their harvesting techniques based on crop conditions, weather patterns, and other factors to maximize crop yield and quality.

Pest and disease detection is a crucial aspect of farming that robotic harvesters can help with. These machines can identify and remove infected crops before they spread to other plants, reducing the need for harmful pesticides and increasing overall crop health. By detecting and managing pests and diseases early on, farmers can prevent significant crop losses and ensure a successful harvest season.

In conclusion, robotic harvesters are a game-changer in the world of agriculture. By incorporating AI applications in agriculture, these advanced machines can revolutionize crop monitoring and management, precision agriculture, pest and disease detection, and more. With the help of robotic harvesters, farmers can optimize crop yields, reduce labor costs, and improve overall efficiency in their farming operations.

Automated Sorting Machines

Automated sorting machines are revolutionizing the way crops are processed and distributed in the agricultural industry. These machines use artificial intelligence to quickly and efficiently sort produce based on size, color, ripeness, and other factors. By automating this process, farmers can save time and labor costs while ensuring that only the highest quality produce makes it to market.

One of the key benefits of automated sorting machines is their ability to increase efficiency in crop monitoring and management. These machines can quickly and accurately assess the quality of crops, allowing farmers to make informed decisions about when to harvest and how to best manage their fields. This real-time data helps farmers optimize their crop yields and maximize profits.

Precision agriculture is another area where automated sorting machines excel. By using AI algorithms, these machines can identify and remove diseased or damaged crops, reducing the spread of pests and diseases and improving overall crop health. This targeted approach to pest and disease detection helps farmers reduce the need for chemical pesticides, leading to more sustainable farming practices.

Livestock monitoring and management is also benefiting from automated sorting machines. These machines can quickly identify and separate animals based on weight, health, and other factors, allowing farmers to provide individualized care and optimize feed and medication schedules. This level of precision in livestock management helps farmers improve animal welfare and increase productivity.

In conclusion, automated sorting machines are transforming the way crops and livestock are managed in agriculture. By harnessing the power of artificial intelligence, these machines are helping farmers increase efficiency, reduce waste, and improve overall crop and livestock health. As the technology continues to advance, we can expect even greater innovations in the field of automated harvesting and sorting in the future.

Post-Harvest Quality Control

Post-harvest quality control is an essential aspect of modern agriculture that ensures the quality and safety of crops after they have been harvested. In the realm of AI applications in agriculture, post-harvest quality control plays a crucial role in optimizing crop yield, reducing waste, and ensuring that consumers receive high-quality products. By utilizing advanced technologies such as machine learning and computer vision, farmers can monitor and manage the quality of their crops more effectively than ever before.

Crop monitoring and management are key components of post-harvest quality control. AI applications allow farmers to track the condition of their crops in real-time, identifying any issues such as pest infestations or disease outbreaks that may affect quality. By using sensors and drones equipped with AI algorithms, farmers can collect data on factors such as moisture levels, temperature, and nutrient content, enabling them to make informed decisions about how to manage their crops for optimal quality.

Precision agriculture is another area where AI applications are revolutionizing post-harvest quality control. By using AI-powered tools to analyze data on soil health, weather patterns, and crop growth, farmers can make precise decisions about when and where to harvest their crops. This level of precision not only ensures high-quality produce but also maximizes crop yield and minimizes waste, resulting in more sustainable farming practices.

Pest and disease detection is a critical component of post-harvest quality control, as infestations can quickly degrade the quality of crops if left unchecked. AI applications can aid in the early detection of pests and diseases by analyzing data from sensors and cameras to identify signs of infestation. By catching these issues early, farmers can take targeted action to mitigate the damage and preserve the quality of their crops.

In conclusion, post-harvest quality control is a vital aspect of modern agriculture that is being transformed by AI applications. By leveraging advanced technologies such as machine learning, computer vision, and data analytics, farmers can monitor and manage the quality of their crops more effectively than ever before. From crop monitoring and management to precision agriculture, pest and disease detection, and more, AI is revolutionizing the way farmers ensure the quality and safety of their produce. By embracing these technologies, farmers can optimize crop yield, reduce waste, and deliver high-quality products to consumers while also promoting sustainability in agriculture.

Chapter 8: Irrigation Management

Smart Irrigation Systems

Smart irrigation systems are revolutionizing the way farmers manage water resources in agriculture. These systems utilize artificial intelligence (AI) technology to optimize irrigation schedules based on real-time data, weather forecasts, and soil moisture levels. By implementing smart irrigation systems, farmers can reduce water waste, improve crop yields, and save time and labor.

One of the key features of smart irrigation systems is the ability to monitor and manage crops more efficiently. Through the use of sensors and data analytics, farmers can track the growth and health of their crops in real-time. This allows them to make informed decisions about when and how much water to apply, leading to healthier plants and higher yields.

Precision agriculture is another area where AI applications in agriculture are making a significant impact. By integrating smart irrigation systems with precision farming techniques, farmers can tailor their irrigation practices to specific areas within a field. This not only conserves water but also ensures that crops receive the right amount of moisture they need to thrive.

In addition to optimizing water usage, smart irrigation systems can also assist in pest and disease detection. By monitoring environmental conditions and crop health indicators, these systems can alert farmers to potential threats before they become widespread. This proactive approach helps farmers take timely action to protect their crops and minimize losses.

Overall, smart irrigation systems are a game-changer for modern agriculture. By harnessing the power of AI technology, farmers can improve crop yields, conserve water resources, and reduce the environmental impact of irrigation practices. As the demand for sustainable farming practices grows, smart irrigation systems will continue to play a crucial role in shaping the future of agriculture.

Soil Moisture Sensors

Soil moisture sensors are an essential tool in modern agriculture, especially in the realm of precision agriculture. These sensors provide farmers with real-time data on the moisture levels in their soil, allowing them to optimize irrigation practices and ensure that crops are receiving the right amount of water. By utilizing soil moisture sensors, farmers can prevent overwatering or underwatering, which can lead to reduced crop yields and increased water usage. This technology is particularly valuable in regions where water is scarce, as it helps farmers make the most efficient use of this precious resource.

In the realm of AI applications in agriculture, soil moisture sensors play a crucial role in crop monitoring and management. By collecting data on soil moisture levels, these sensors provide valuable insights into the health and growth of crops. This information can then be used to adjust irrigation schedules, fertilization practices, and other factors that impact crop growth. By integrating soil moisture sensors with AI algorithms, farmers can make more informed decisions about how to optimize crop production and maximize yields.

In addition to crop monitoring and management, soil moisture sensors are also useful for pest and disease detection. By monitoring soil moisture levels, farmers can identify areas of their fields that may be more susceptible to pests or diseases. This early detection allows farmers to take proactive measures to prevent infestations and protect their crops. By utilizing AI algorithms to analyze the data collected by soil moisture sensors, farmers can even predict potential pest outbreaks and take preemptive action to mitigate their impact.

Soil moisture sensors are also valuable tools for soil health analysis. By monitoring moisture levels in the soil, farmers can assess the overall health of their soil and identify areas that may be lacking in nutrients or experiencing other issues. This information can then be used to tailor fertilization practices and other soil management techniques to improve soil health and maximize crop yields. By leveraging AI applications in conjunction with soil moisture sensors, farmers can gain deeper insights into their soil health and make more informed decisions about how to improve it.

Overall, soil moisture sensors are a critical component of modern agriculture, particularly in the realm of precision agriculture. By providing real-time data on soil moisture levels, these sensors enable farmers to optimize their irrigation practices, monitor crop health, detect pests and diseases, analyze soil health, and make informed decisions about how to improve crop yields. By integrating soil moisture sensors with AI applications, farmers can leverage this technology to revolutionize their farming practices and achieve greater efficiency, sustainability, and profitability.

Drip Irrigation Technology

Drip irrigation technology is a crucial aspect of modern agriculture that utilizes AI applications to optimize water usage and increase crop yield. This technology involves delivering water directly to the roots of plants through a network of tubes and emitters, ensuring that each plant receives the right amount of water at the right time. By incorporating AI algorithms, farmers can monitor and adjust the irrigation system based on real-time data such as soil moisture levels, weather conditions, and crop water requirements.

One of the key benefits of drip irrigation technology is its ability to improve water efficiency in agriculture. By delivering water directly to the roots of plants, this technology reduces water wastage and minimizes evaporation, leading to significant water savings. AI applications further enhance water efficiency by analyzing data from sensors and weather forecasts to automatically adjust irrigation schedules and optimize water usage. This not only conserves water resources but also reduces operating costs for farmers.

In addition to water efficiency, drip irrigation technology also plays a crucial role in crop monitoring and management. AI-powered sensors can collect data on plant health, growth patterns, and nutrient levels, allowing farmers to make informed decisions about crop management practices. By integrating this data with irrigation systems, farmers can tailor their watering schedules to meet the specific needs of different crops, resulting in healthier plants and higher yields.

Furthermore, drip irrigation technology combined with AI applications enables precision agriculture, a farming approach that utilizes data-driven insights to optimize crop production. By analyzing data on soil health, weather conditions, and crop performance, farmers can make precise decisions about irrigation, fertilization, and pest control strategies. This level of precision not only improves crop quality and yield but also minimizes environmental impact by reducing the use of chemicals and water.

Overall, drip irrigation technology is a vital component of the future of farming, empowered by AI applications that revolutionize irrigation management. From water efficiency and crop monitoring to precision agriculture and crop yield optimization, this technology offers numerous benefits for farmers looking to maximize productivity and sustainability in their operations. By embracing drip irrigation technology and harnessing the power of AI, farmers can unlock new opportunities for growth and innovation in the agricultural industry.

Chapter 9: Weather Forecasting and Crop Prediction

Weather Data Analytics

Weather data analytics plays a crucial role in modern agriculture, especially when combined with AI applications. By utilizing advanced technologies to analyze weather patterns and data, farmers can make more informed decisions about their crops, ultimately leading to better yields and increased profitability. In this subchapter, we will explore how weather data analytics can revolutionize the way we approach farming and how it can be integrated with AI applications to maximize efficiency and productivity.

Crop monitoring and management is one area where weather data analytics can make a significant impact. By tracking weather patterns and using predictive analytics, farmers can better understand how their crops are being affected by temperature, humidity, and precipitation. This information allows farmers to make adjustments to their growing practices in real-time, ensuring that their crops are receiving the optimal conditions for growth and development.

Precision agriculture is another area where weather data analytics can be incredibly beneficial. By combining weather data with satellite imagery and other sources of information, farmers can create detailed maps of their fields that highlight areas of potential concern. This allows farmers to target specific areas for treatment, such as irrigation or fertilization, resulting in a more efficient use of resources and better crop yields.

Pest and disease detection can also be improved through the use of weather data analytics. By monitoring weather patterns and analyzing historical data, farmers can predict when certain pests and diseases are most likely to strike. This information allows farmers to take preemptive measures to protect their crops, reducing the need for costly treatments and minimizing the risk of crop loss.

In conclusion, weather data analytics is a powerful tool that can revolutionize the way we approach farming. By utilizing advanced technologies to analyze weather patterns and data, farmers can make more informed decisions about their crops, leading to better yields and increased profitability. When integrated with AI applications, weather data analytics can take agriculture to new heights, ensuring that farmers are equipped with the knowledge they need to succeed in an ever-changing environment.

Climate Prediction Models

Climate prediction models are a crucial tool in the realm of AI applications in agriculture, as they provide valuable insights into weather patterns and trends that can significantly impact crop production. By utilizing advanced algorithms and data analytics, these models can accurately predict various climatic conditions such as temperature, rainfall, humidity, and wind speed, allowing farmers to make informed decisions about crop planting, irrigation, and pest control.

One of the key benefits of climate prediction models is their ability to help farmers anticipate and prepare for extreme weather events, such as droughts, floods, and heatwaves. By analyzing historical weather data and incorporating real-time information from sensors and satellites, these models can forecast the likelihood of such events occurring in a particular region, enabling farmers to take proactive measures to protect their crops and minimize potential losses.

Moreover, climate prediction models play a vital role in crop monitoring and management by providing detailed insights into how different weather conditions impact plant growth and development. By analyzing factors such as temperature, rainfall, and sunlight exposure, these models can help farmers optimize their planting schedules, irrigation practices, and fertilizer applications to ensure maximum yields and quality.

In addition, climate prediction models are instrumental in precision agriculture, as they enable farmers to tailor their cultivation practices to suit specific environmental conditions. By combining weather forecasting data with crop growth models and satellite imagery, farmers can create customized management plans for each field, optimizing resource usage and minimizing environmental impact.

Overall, climate prediction models are an invaluable tool for modern farming practices, helping farmers make data-driven decisions that enhance crop productivity, sustainability, and profitability. By harnessing the power of AI technology, these models have the potential to revolutionize the way we approach agriculture, ensuring food security and environmental stewardship for future generations.

Crop Yield Forecasting

Crop yield forecasting is a crucial aspect of modern agriculture that can greatly benefit from the application of artificial intelligence (AI) technology. By utilizing AI algorithms and data analytics, farmers can predict the potential yield of their crops with a high degree of accuracy. This allows them to make informed decisions about crop management practices, resource allocation, and marketing strategies.

One of the key benefits of crop yield forecasting using AI is the ability to optimize crop production and maximize yields. By analyzing historical data, weather patterns, soil conditions, and other relevant factors, AI algorithms can provide farmers with valuable insights into how to improve crop yields. This can help farmers reduce waste, increase efficiency, and ultimately boost their profitability.

In addition to optimizing crop yields, AI-powered crop yield forecasting can also help farmers better manage their resources. By accurately predicting crop yields, farmers can adjust their irrigation, fertilization, and pest control strategies to ensure optimal crop health and productivity. This can lead to cost savings, reduced environmental impact, and improved sustainability in agriculture.

Furthermore, AI applications in crop yield forecasting can help farmers mitigate risks associated with weather variability, pests, and diseases. By providing early warnings of potential threats to crop yields, AI technology enables farmers to take proactive measures to protect their crops and minimize losses. This can help farmers maintain a stable and reliable food supply while reducing the need for costly interventions.

Overall, crop yield forecasting using AI technology holds great promise for the future of agriculture. By harnessing the power of data and advanced analytics, farmers can make more informed decisions, optimize crop production, and ensure the sustainability of their operations. As AI technology continues to advance, we can expect to see even greater benefits in terms of crop monitoring, management, and overall productivity in agriculture.

Chapter 10: Crop Yield Optimization

Yield Prediction Models

Yield prediction models are powerful tools in the realm of precision agriculture, allowing farmers to make informed decisions about crop management and optimize their overall yield. These models utilize advanced algorithms and machine learning techniques to analyze a variety of factors, such as weather patterns, soil health, and historical crop data, to predict future yields with a high degree of accuracy. By utilizing these models, farmers can better plan their planting and harvesting schedules, as well as make adjustments to their irrigation and fertilization practices to maximize crop productivity.

One key benefit of yield prediction models is their ability to help farmers mitigate risks and uncertainties associated with farming. By providing accurate forecasts of crop yields, farmers can anticipate potential challenges such as pest outbreaks, droughts, or other environmental factors that may impact their harvest. This allows farmers to take proactive measures to protect their crops and ensure a successful harvest, ultimately increasing their overall profitability.

In addition to helping farmers optimize their crop yields, yield prediction models also play a crucial role in supply chain management and logistics in agriculture. By accurately forecasting crop yields, farmers can better plan their distribution strategies, ensuring that they have the right amount of produce available to meet market demands. This can help reduce waste and spoilage, as well as improve the overall efficiency of the agricultural supply chain.

Furthermore, yield prediction models can also be used to optimize crop yield in a sustainable manner. By analyzing data on soil health, weather patterns, and crop rotation practices, farmers can identify areas where improvements can be made to increase productivity while minimizing environmental impact. This holistic approach to crop management not only benefits farmers in terms of profitability but also promotes long-term sustainability in agriculture.

Overall, yield prediction models are a valuable tool for farmers looking to leverage the power of AI applications in agriculture. By harnessing the predictive capabilities of these models, farmers can make more informed decisions about their crop management practices, optimize their yields, and improve the efficiency and sustainability of their farming operations. As technology continues to advance, the potential for yield prediction models to revolutionize the future of farming is immense, offering endless possibilities for innovation and growth in the agricultural sector.

Crop Growth Simulations

Crop growth simulations are a vital component of precision agriculture, allowing farmers to predict and optimize crop yields based on various factors such as weather conditions, soil health, and pest infestations. By utilizing artificial intelligence (AI) applications, farmers can simulate different growth scenarios and make informed decisions to maximize productivity and minimize losses.

One of the key benefits of crop growth simulations is the ability to monitor and manage crops in real-time. AI-powered tools can analyze data from sensors, drones, and satellite imagery to provide farmers with detailed insights into the health and growth of their crops. This information can help farmers identify potential issues early on and take proactive measures to mitigate risks and improve overall crop health.

In addition to monitoring and managing crops, AI applications can also assist in pest and disease detection. By analyzing data from various sources, such as images of plants and soil samples, AI algorithms can identify signs of pests and diseases before they become widespread. This early detection allows farmers to take targeted actions, such as applying pesticides or implementing crop rotation strategies, to prevent further damage to their crops.

Livestock monitoring and management is another area where AI applications can have a significant impact. By using sensors and wearable devices, farmers can track the health and behavior of their livestock in real-time. AI algorithms can analyze this data to detect signs of illness or distress, allowing farmers to provide timely care and improve the overall well-being of their animals.

Overall, crop growth simulations powered by AI have the potential to revolutionize the way farmers approach agriculture. By leveraging advanced technologies to monitor, manage, and optimize crop production, farmers can increase yields, reduce costs, and contribute to a more sustainable and efficient food system. As the agriculture industry continues to embrace AI applications, we can expect to see even greater advancements in crop yield optimization, supply chain management, and overall productivity in the years to come.

Crop Rotation Strategies

In the world of agriculture, crop rotation strategies play a crucial role in maintaining soil fertility, preventing pest and disease outbreaks, and maximizing crop yields. With the advancement of technology, artificial intelligence (AI) applications have revolutionized the way farmers approach crop rotation. By utilizing AI algorithms and data analytics, farmers can now make more informed decisions when it comes to planning their crop rotation strategies.

One of the key benefits of using AI in crop rotation is the ability to analyze large amounts of data to identify the most optimal crop sequence for a particular field. By taking into account factors such as soil health, weather patterns, and pest history, AI algorithms can recommend the best crop rotation strategy to maximize yields and minimize risks. This level of precision and accuracy is essential for modern farmers looking to optimize their farming practices and increase profitability.

Crop monitoring and management are also greatly enhanced by AI applications in agriculture. Through the use of drones, satellites, and sensors, farmers can gather real-time data on crop health, growth patterns, and nutrient levels. This data can then be used to make informed decisions about when to plant, water, fertilize, or harvest crops, leading to more efficient and sustainable farming practices.

Precision agriculture is another area where AI applications are making a significant impact. By using AI-powered tools such as automated tractors, drones, and sensors, farmers can precisely apply fertilizers, pesticides, and water to specific areas of their fields, reducing waste and increasing crop yields. This level of precision is essential for sustainable farming practices and ensuring the long-term health of the soil and environment.

Overall, AI applications in agriculture are transforming the way farmers approach crop rotation strategies, crop monitoring and management, precision agriculture, pest and disease detection, livestock monitoring and management, soil health analysis, automated harvesting and sorting, irrigation management, weather forecasting and crop prediction, crop yield optimization, and supply chain management and logistics. By harnessing the power of AI, farmers can make more informed decisions, increase efficiency, and ultimately improve the sustainability and profitability of their farming operations.

Chapter 11: Supply Chain Management and Logistics in Agriculture

Traceability Systems

Traceability systems play a crucial role in the agricultural industry, especially with the growing importance of food safety and sustainability. These systems allow for the tracking and tracing of agricultural products throughout the supply chain, from farm to table. In the context of AI applications in agriculture, traceability systems are becoming increasingly sophisticated, utilizing advanced technologies to ensure the integrity and transparency of the food supply.

One key aspect of traceability systems in agriculture is crop monitoring and management. AI-powered sensors and imaging technologies can provide real-time data on crop health and growth, allowing farmers to make informed decisions about irrigation, fertilization, and pest control. This level of precision and efficiency is essential for maximizing yields and minimizing environmental impact.

Precision agriculture is another area where traceability systems are making a significant impact. By integrating data from GPS, sensors, and drones, farmers can create detailed maps of their fields and tailor their farming practices to specific areas. This targeted approach not only improves crop productivity but also reduces input costs and minimizes waste.

Pest and disease detection is another critical application of traceability systems in agriculture. By using AI algorithms to analyze data from sensors and cameras, farmers can quickly identify and respond to potential threats to their crops. Early detection is key to preventing widespread damage and ensuring the overall health of the farm.

In conclusion, traceability systems are revolutionizing the way we approach agriculture, providing farmers with the tools they need to make informed decisions and optimize their operations. From crop monitoring and management to pest and disease detection, these systems are transforming the industry and helping to ensure a sustainable and secure food supply for the future.

Real-Time Inventory Management

Real-time inventory management is a crucial aspect of modern agriculture, especially with the advent of AI applications in the industry. With the help of advanced technologies, farmers can now monitor and manage their crop inventory in real-time, ensuring optimal efficiency and productivity. This subchapter will delve into the various ways in which AI is revolutionizing inventory management in agriculture, providing valuable insights for those interested in the future of farming.

One of the key benefits of real-time inventory management is the ability to accurately track and monitor crop levels at any given time. AI-powered sensors and monitoring systems can provide real-time data on crop growth, yield, and storage conditions, allowing farmers to make informed decisions on when to harvest, store, or sell their produce. This level of precision and accuracy can help farmers optimize their crop yield and maximize profits.

Precision agriculture is another area where real-time inventory management plays a crucial role. By using AI to monitor and analyze crop data in real-time, farmers can identify areas of their fields that require attention, such as pest infestations or nutrient deficiencies. This enables them to take immediate action to address these issues, leading to healthier crops and higher yields.

Furthermore, real-time inventory management can also help farmers detect and prevent pest and disease outbreaks before they spread and cause significant damage to their crops. AI-powered systems can analyze crop data and identify early warning signs of potential threats, allowing farmers to implement targeted interventions to protect their crops. This proactive approach can save farmers time and money, while also reducing the need for harmful pesticides.

In conclusion, real-time inventory management is a game-changer for modern agriculture, thanks to the advancements in AI applications. By leveraging these technologies, farmers can improve crop monitoring and management, precision agriculture, pest and disease detection, livestock monitoring and management, soil health analysis, automated harvesting and sorting, irrigation management, weather forecasting and crop prediction, crop yield optimization, and supply chain management and logistics in agriculture. With real-time inventory management, farmers can optimize their operations, increase efficiency, and ultimately, achieve sustainable and profitable farming practices.

Transportation Optimization

Transportation optimization is a key aspect of AI applications in agriculture that can greatly improve efficiency and reduce costs for farmers. By utilizing AI algorithms and data analytics, farmers can optimize their transportation routes, schedules, and logistics to ensure timely delivery of goods and materials. This can help minimize fuel consumption, reduce idle time, and increase overall productivity on the farm.

One of the main benefits of transportation optimization in agriculture is the ability to streamline the movement of goods from farm to market. By using AI to analyze real-time data on road conditions, traffic patterns, and weather forecasts, farmers can make informed decisions about the best routes to take and the most efficient times to transport their products. This can help reduce delays, minimize spoilage, and ultimately increase profitability for farmers.

In addition to improving the efficiency of transportation routes, AI can also assist with fleet management and monitoring. By equipping vehicles with sensors and GPS technology, farmers can track the location, speed, and performance of their vehicles in real-time. This can help prevent breakdowns, optimize maintenance schedules, and ensure that vehicles are operating at peak efficiency.

Furthermore, transportation optimization can also play a crucial role in supply chain management and logistics in agriculture. By integrating AI into inventory management systems, farmers can better track and forecast demand for their products, optimize storage and distribution processes, and minimize waste throughout the supply chain. This can help ensure that products reach consumers in a timely manner and maintain high quality standards.

Overall, transportation optimization is a powerful tool that can help farmers leverage the benefits of AI applications in agriculture to improve efficiency, reduce costs, and increase profitability. By harnessing the power of AI algorithms and data analytics, farmers can optimize their transportation routes, fleet management, and supply chain logistics to ensure successful and sustainable farming practices in the future.

Chapter 12: Conclusion

Future Trends in AI Applications in Agriculture

The future of agriculture lies in the integration of artificial intelligence (AI) applications to enhance productivity, efficiency, and sustainability. In this subchapter, we will explore the upcoming trends in AI applications in agriculture that are revolutionizing the way we cultivate crops and manage livestock. From crop monitoring and management to precision agriculture, pest and disease detection, and soil health analysis, AI is paving the way for a more data-driven and informed approach to farming.

One of the key trends in AI applications in agriculture is the use of crop monitoring and management systems. These systems utilize drones, satellites, and sensors to collect real-time data on crop health, growth, and environmental conditions. By analyzing this data, farmers can make informed decisions about irrigation, fertilization, and pest control, leading to higher yields and reduced input costs. In the future, we can expect to see even more advanced AI algorithms that can predict crop growth and optimize management practices.

Precision agriculture is another area where AI is making a significant impact. By using machine learning algorithms to analyze data from sensors and drones, farmers can create detailed maps of their fields and tailor inputs such as water, fertilizers, and pesticides to specific areas. This not only increases the efficiency of resource use but also minimizes environmental impact. As AI technology advances, we can anticipate even more precise and targeted farming practices that optimize yields while minimizing waste.

Pest and disease detection is another crucial area where AI is transforming agriculture. By analyzing images of crops or using sensors to detect early signs of disease or infestation, AI systems can alert farmers to potential threats before they become widespread. This early detection can save crops and reduce the need for chemical treatments, leading to healthier plants and higher yields. In the future, we can expect to see AI systems that can not only detect but also predict outbreaks of pests and diseases, allowing for proactive management strategies.

Livestock monitoring and management is also benefiting from AI applications. By using sensors and wearable devices to track the health and behavior of animals, farmers can ensure optimal conditions for their livestock and detect signs of illness or distress early on. AI algorithms can analyze this data to provide insights into animal health, nutrition, and reproduction, leading to improved productivity and welfare. In the future, we can expect to see AI systems that can predict disease outbreaks, optimize feed formulations, and even automate tasks such as feeding and milking.

In conclusion, the future of farming is bright with the integration of AI applications in agriculture. From crop monitoring and management to precision agriculture, pest and disease detection, and livestock monitoring, AI is revolutionizing every aspect of the farming process. By harnessing the power of data and machine learning algorithms, farmers can make more informed decisions, increase productivity, and reduce environmental impact. As technology continues to advance, we can expect even more innovative AI solutions that will shape the future of agriculture for years to come.

Challenges and Opportunities in AgTech

In the ever-evolving field of agriculture, the integration of AI applications presents both challenges and opportunities for farmers and industry professionals alike. As technology continues to advance, there is a growing need for innovative solutions to address issues such as climate change, population growth, and food security. With the help of AI, farmers can optimize their operations and maximize crop yields while minimizing environmental impact.

One of the key challenges in implementing AI applications in agriculture is the initial cost of investment. Many farmers may be hesitant to adopt new technologies due to the perceived high costs associated with purchasing and implementing AI systems. However, the long-term benefits of increased efficiency, reduced labor costs, and improved crop yields can outweigh the initial investment, making it a worthwhile endeavor for those looking to stay competitive in the industry.

On the other hand, the opportunities presented by AI applications in agriculture are vast. From crop monitoring and management to precision agriculture and pest and disease detection, AI technology has the potential to revolutionize the way we approach farming. By utilizing data analytics and machine learning algorithms, farmers can make more informed decisions about planting, harvesting, and crop treatment, leading to higher yields and better quality produce.

In addition to improving crop management, AI applications also play a crucial role in livestock monitoring and management. By utilizing sensors and data analysis, farmers can track the health and well-being of their animals, ensuring optimal conditions for growth and productivity. Furthermore, AI technology can be used to analyze soil health and optimize irrigation management, leading to more sustainable farming practices and improved environmental outcomes.

Overall, the future of farming is bright with the integration of AI applications in agriculture. From automated harvesting and sorting to weather forecasting and crop prediction, AI technology offers endless possibilities for optimizing crop yields, improving supply chain management, and enhancing overall efficiency in the agricultural industry. By embracing these challenges and opportunities, farmers can stay ahead of the curve and continue to meet the growing demands of a rapidly changing world.

The Impact of AI on the Future of Farming

Artificial Intelligence (AI) is revolutionizing the field of agriculture, with a wide range of applications that are transforming the way farmers manage their crops and livestock. From crop monitoring and management to precision agriculture, pest and disease detection, and soil health analysis, AI is helping farmers make more informed decisions and optimize their operations for increased productivity and sustainability.

One of the key benefits of AI in farming is its ability to provide real-time data and insights that can help farmers make more accurate and timely decisions. By using AI-powered tools for crop monitoring and management, farmers can track the health and growth of their crops, identify areas that need attention, and optimize their irrigation and fertilization practices for maximum yield. This not only improves crop quality and quantity but also reduces waste and environmental impact.

Precision agriculture is another area where AI is making a significant impact. By using drones, sensors, and other smart technologies, farmers can gather data on soil conditions, weather patterns, and crop health to make more precise decisions about planting, fertilizing, and harvesting. This not only improves efficiency and profitability but also reduces the use of resources such as water, fertilizer, and pesticides, leading to a more sustainable farming practice.

AI is also playing a crucial role in pest and disease detection, helping farmers identify and treat potential threats before they spread and cause significant damage. By analyzing data from sensors, drones, and other sources, AI can detect early signs of infestation or disease, allowing farmers to take proactive measures to protect their crops and minimize losses. This not only saves time and money but also reduces the need for harmful pesticides and chemicals.

In addition to crop management, AI is also being used in livestock monitoring and management to track the health, behavior, and productivity of animals. By using sensors, wearables, and other technologies, farmers can monitor the well-being of their livestock, detect any signs of illness or distress, and optimize feeding and breeding practices for improved performance. This not only improves animal welfare but also enhances farm productivity and profitability.

Overall, the impact of AI on the future of farming is undeniable. With its ability to provide real-time data, insights, and automated decision-making, AI is helping farmers optimize their operations, increase productivity, and reduce waste and environmental impact. As technology continues to evolve and improve, the potential for AI applications in agriculture is limitless, offering endless possibilities for innovation and sustainable growth in the farming industry.

www.ingramcontent.com/pod-product-compliance
Lightning Source LLC
Chambersburg PA
CBHW082224220526
45470CB00010B/3304